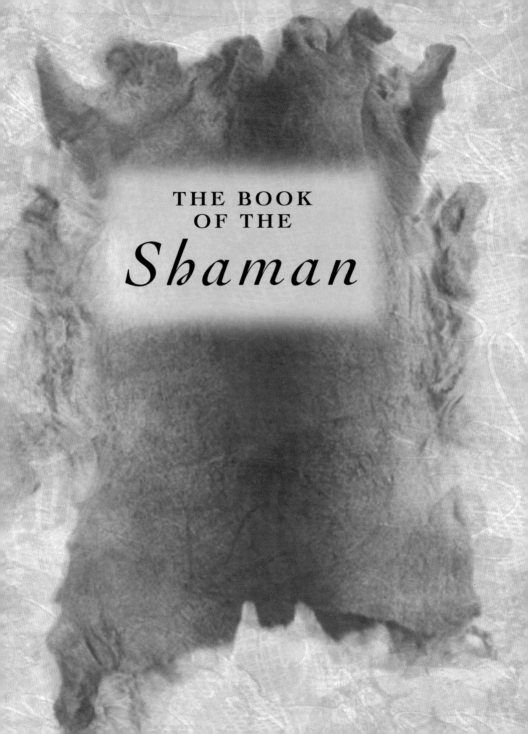

THE BOOK OF THE
Shaman

THE BOOK
OF THE
Shaman

WALK THE ANCIENT PATH OF
THE SHAMAN AND FIND INNER PEACE

NICHOLAS WOOD

BARRON'S

A QUARTO BOOK

First edition for the United States, its territories
and dependencies, and Canada published in 2001
by Barron's Educational Series, Inc.

All inquiries should be addressed to:
Barron's Educational Series, Inc.
250 Wireless Boulevard
Hauppauge, NY 11788
http://www.barronseduc.com

Library of Congress Catalog Card Number: 00-104870

International Standard Book Number: 0-7641-5367-6

Conceived, designed, and produced by
Quarto Publishing plc
The Old Brewery
6 Blundell Street
London N7 9BH

QUAR.DEV

Senior editor: Michelle Pickering
Senior art editor: Sally Bond
Assistant art director: Penny Cobb
Editor: Mary Senechal
Designer & montage artist: Caroline Grimshaw
Photographer: Pat Aithie, Martin Norris, Colin Bowling
Picture researcher: Laurent Boubounelle
Indexer: Dorothy Frame

Art director: Moira Clinch
Publisher: Piers Spence

Manufactured by Regent Publishing Services Ltd,
Hong Kong
Printed by Midas Printing Ltd, China

9 8 7 6 5 4 3 2 1

Contents

Chapter One

THE WORLD OF THE
Shaman

Chapter Two

THE TOOLS OF THE
Shaman

Chapter Three

WALKING YOUR OWN
Path

INTRODUCTION

WE ARE NOT HUMAN BEINGS BY ACCIDENT OR BY RIGHT; WE ARE MERELY TWO-LEGGED CREATURES. BECOMING A HUMAN BEING IN THE TRUEST SENSE OF THE WORD IS A JOURNEY WE CAN UNDERTAKE WITH JOY—OR A PATH WE IGNORE AT OUR PERIL.

The world has changed so much in the last two hundred years and change is accelerating so fast that we can feel dizzy just trying to keep up. Since the Industrial Revolution, we have gone from being a largely rural society to a society in which many of us rarely leave an urban environment. We experience the shifting seasons mostly by glimpsing the weather when we step outside our workplace or visit the supermarket, and by variations in the products we find on the shelves.

THE ENDURING EARTH

It is a world that our ancestors could scarcely have imagined, but beneath our feet—beneath the concrete and the steel, the stone and the gravel—is the earth. It has always been there, and we earth people walk upon it. We can choose to walk on it in contempt, or we can walk on it in a sacred way. Deep beneath the streets of New York, London, or Paris, our ancestors walked long ago and made a sacred connection with the earth. They held ceremonies and danced, called to the spirits, prayed, and found sacred enrichment.

ANIMISM

Modern life can make the spiritual world seem remote and alien, yet most people still pick up pinecones in the park, or marvel at the shape of a seashell. There is an instinctive human need to wonder about the world and to communicate with it. A spiritual awareness of the world, a respectful acknowledgment of its total aliveness and wonder, is known as animism. Animists believe that a mountain has a spirit, that the earth has a spirit, and that a tree also has a spirit. They may speak to a thunderstorm or an ocean; they may talk to a car. Animism is the root of all the spiritual traditions on earth. It was the way our ancestors saw the world, and, deep down, it remains part of our nature.

The simple riches of the natural world are always there for us.

The world of nature is a world of spirits that move powerfully all around us.

SHAMANISM

Animism is the principle behind the ancient spiritual path of shamanism. A shaman is a person who is profoundly aware that the world is alive with spirits and spiritual energy, and who does something with that knowledge. He or she recognizes that the spirits of the mountains, the rivers, the ancestors, and all of the other spirits who share our world are available to us here and now. Shamans study the ways of the "old people" and of those who have gone before us, and find ways to communicate with the spirits all around them. They learn to travel among the spirits by entering into a trance state. They ask the spirits for help with healing, and learn to understand and assist the dance of life, the great dance of which we are all part.

THE WAYS OF THE SHAMAN

This book cannot turn you into a shaman. Shamans dedicate their lives to their vocation. They sacrifice themselves for their people and spend many years acquiring knowledge and skills that take even longer to comprehend. But this book can open a door into the shaman's world and show you how to use some of the shaman's ways. Those ways are not meant to give you power over others, or to bring you material success; they are meant to bring you into closer contact with the dance in which all things move, to deepen your awareness of it, to allow you to experience the wonder of the seas and the moon, the tree and the eagle— and to become a more complete human being.

A traditional Mongolian shaman understands the relationship between the spirits and human beings.

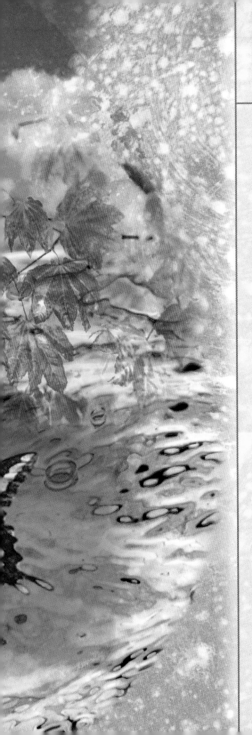

CHAPTER ONE

THE WORLD
OF THE
Shaman

For the shaman, everything is alive and possesses a spirit. Everything is part of creation and equal to all other parts. The shaman is a two-legged person, just as there are four-legged people, many-legged people, swimming people, flying people, and myriad other beings who live between Grandmother Earth and Grandfather Sky.

The shaman gains this knowledge from the spirits and from the teaching of other shamans. But the spirits are the primary source; they plant the seeds that the older shamans helped to nurture during the shaman's training.

The people look to the shaman for help—in healing the sick, in finding those who are lost, in observing the cycle of the year, and in knowing the right times to perform the movements in the sacred dance of which they are part. Shamans serve the people and the spirits. They form a bridge between the two.

WHAT IS A SHAMAN?

A SHAMAN CAN BE BROADLY DEFINED AS A PERSON OF EITHER SEX WHO CAN PERCEIVE THE WORLD OF SPIRITS, AND BY ENTERING A TRANCE, JOURNEY TO ANOTHER REALITY, TO COMMUNICATE WITH ITS INHABITANTS, AND TO GAIN SPIRITUAL KNOWLEDGE.

The word shaman comes from the language of the Tungus tribe of Siberia, and means a healer and magician. Siberia held a long-standing fascination for some in Russia, and there were expeditions and royal excursions there for several centuries. Writers in the late 19th century used the word shaman to describe the tribal healers of the region, and the term slowly spread from Russian literature to be applied to similar tribal spiritual systems throughout the world.

RESPECT AND FEAR

We tend to think of a shaman as a tribal figure, living among the people as their healer or priest, and conserving tribal lore. This is partly correct; shamans are often considered

holy, but their relationship with the tribe depends upon the cultural context. Some accept and honor their shamans, giving them a place among the people and treating them with importance. Other cultures fear the shamans, who live apart from the main tribal group and are only visited when people need their help.

A Siberian shaman and a young member of the tribe, who perhaps one day will become the people's shaman.

19th-century
engraving of
a Mongolian
shaman
performing
a ceremony.

SACRED TECHNICIANS

Shamans usually possess expertise in illness and healing, which may or may not include a considerable knowledge of herbs and plants. They are likely to be skilled in performing ceremonies to ensure good hunting or harvest, and to be experienced in the rituals surrounding birth, puberty, marriage, and death. They may also be responsible for recording the passage of time.

Most important of all, they act as a bridge between the everyday and the sacred, the world of two-legged beings and the world of the spirits. They often facilitate the annual ceremonies that bind the world of humans and the world of the spirits. The shamans are sacred technicians.

Living in the natural world requires a skilled relationship with all that is around you.

SHAMANS THROUGHOUT
THE WORLD

SHAMANS HAVE A KNOWLEDGE OF THE SPIRITUAL STRUCTURE OF LIFE. THEY SEE THAT HUMANS HAVE A RELATIONSHIP—BOTH SPIRITUAL AND CORPORAL—WITH ALL THE OTHER BEINGS IN THE WORLD, AND CANNOT LIVE IN ISOLATION FROM THEM. SHAMANS WERE THE FIRST PEOPLE TO WORK ACTIVELY WITH THE SACRED, THE FIRST PEOPLE TO ENTER INTO A SACRED DIALOGUE WITH CREATION.

AN ANCIENT TRADITION

Shamanism has existed for tens of thousands of years. In the Mojave Desert of California are rock carvings dated to around 10,000 B.C. They use symbols that Native Americans still use. When the carvings were made, around 12,000 years ago, the shamanic tradition from which they came was already well established, and was possibly already ancient.

A CENTRAL BELIEF

The world works a certain way: the sun rises, the sun sets, people live, people die, sometimes food is plentiful, sometimes food is scarce, people are healthy, or they get sick. For many hundreds of generations, shamans have listened to the world, watched the world, and heeded the communications of the spirits.

The world is fundamentally similar wherever you live. The weather may be warmer or colder, but there are many basic conditions that people everywhere share. Is it any wonder, then, that shamanic traditions throughout the world have many insights in common? That is not to underestimate cultural variations; there may be many differences between a Mongolian shaman, who blends his tradition with Tibetan Buddhism, and a Mayan "day keeper" from Mexico, who mixes his traditions with a little Catholic Christianity, but beneath these surface manifestations, the understandings that each possesses about the sacred nature of the world have many similarities.

Ancient rock art, such as these paintings from Utah in the United States, gives us a glimpse of a shaman's eye view of the world.

15

SPANNING THE EARTH

Tribal people throughout the world share one central belief: they all see the world as being deeply alive. They share a sense of being connected to the world, stitched into the sacred fabric of creation—an important thread in the way things are. And with this perception comes the need for a person who can communicate with the world: the shaman. Our ancestors were people like us, and they knew that the world was alive. As a Native American remarked, "You guys had these teachings once, but you lost them!" Now is the time to get them back.

NORTH AMERICA

From Siberia and the Far East, shamanism spread across the Bering Strait to Alaska, and on into Canada and Greenland. Many of the Native American tribes of North America have a shamanic view of the world.

CENTRAL AMERICA

There was a deeply animistic and shamanic flavor to the spiritual understanding of the Golden Sun empires of Mexico and Central America, such as the Aztecs and the Maya.

SOUTH AMERICA

An animistic and shamanic awareness is found in the spiritual beliefs of South America, whether in the green rain forests, in the cold mountain heights, in the deserts of the west coast, or in the near tundra of the very southernmost tip.

16

EUROPE

From western Siberia, shamanic elements spilled over into northern Europe, and on down into the warmer climates of central Europe. In Britain and other parts of Europe, there are numerous standing stones, stone circles, and churches built on sacred sites far older than Christianity. The people who built them shared much with the Siberians, the Native Americans, and the Aborigines.

SIBERIA, RUSSIA, AND THE FAR EAST

Shamanism occurs throughout Siberia, and in southern Siberia, Mongolia, and China it formed a mutually enriching fusion with Buddhism. Traces of a shamanic culture can be found in the islands between Russia, China, and Japan.

THE MIDDLE EAST

In classical times, the Middle East experienced contact with shamanic tribes sweeping in from the steppes of Siberia.

AFRICA, THE PACIFIC, AND AUSTRALIA

Shamanism also exists in Africa, the Pacific islands, and Australia. The culture of the Aborigines of Australia is rich with shamanic spiritual wisdom.

WALKING WITH THE SPIRITS

IN THE SHAMAN'S WORLD, WHEREVER YOU ARE AND WHATEVER YOU ARE DOING, YOU ARE SURROUNDED BY SPIRITS. ALL SO-CALLED LIVING THINGS, SUCH AS PLANTS AND ANIMALS, HAVE SPIRITS, BUT SO DO THE THINGS WE NORMALLY REGARD AS INANIMATE, SUCH AS ROCKS AND RIVERS. EVERYTHING IS PART OF THE FABRIC OF CREATION, AND SO EVERYTHING HAS A SPIRIT.

There are also spirits of beings who do not manifest themselves in the physical world. These include the spirits of ancestors and of totem animals, the spirits of illness, celestial spirits, such as the spirit of the underworld or the sky, the spirits of the "four directions," the spirit of a building, or of the shaman's drum.

A PRAGMATIC SPIRITUALITY

In this world of spirits, we walk as part of the sacred dance of all things. All beings walk in this world, but it is the shaman who learns to interact with the spirits. Shamans learn the songs that need to be sung and the ceremonies that need to be performed. Shamans do all this because the performance of these acts creates a "right relationship" with everything. It brings a harmony and a beauty to the world. And they do it, because it works—the spirits do help to heal, the spirits do help to hunt. Shamanism is a pragmatic spirituality.

HOME FOR THE SOUL

We rely on our knowledge and sophisticated science when things go wrong, and many modern accomplishments are undoubtedly wonderful. But the spirits have helped people longer than machines have, and communicating with them feeds the soul far more than the latest technological advance could ever do. Deep inside of us, when we follow the ancient ways, we are coming home.

Shamanic belief is centered around the fact that we are all part of a sacred circle that contains all things.

ALL THINGS ARE RELATED

IN THE BEGINNING WAS THE EVERYTHING, THE EVERYTHING THAT WAS MALE AND THE EVERYTHING THAT WAS FEMALE, THE EVERYTHING THAT WAS HOT AND THE EVERYTHING THAT WAS COLD, WAS UP AND DOWN, WAS DARK AND LIGHT—THE GREAT-GRANDFATHER AND THE GREAT-GRANDMOTHER OF ALL THINGS.

THE WEB OF LIFE

And these two danced together, and as they danced, they made love, and gave birth to the first born: the sun. And they danced and made love again, and gave birth to the second born: the earth. And the children of the Great-Grandparents, the sun and the earth, made love and their child was the Sacred Plant people. They made love again, and gave birth to the Sacred Animals, and again they made love, and gave birth to the Sacred Humans. That is why we are all related.

This sense of a connection between all beings is shared by a large number of tribal cultures. In many Native American spiritual traditions, especially that of the Lakota, the words "for all my relations" are spoken in ceremony. The words are a sacred prayer, a way of saying thank you to all that exists for the gift of life. When a ceremony is performed, it is enacted for all of our relations, for the health of all beings. In the words attributed to the Native American orator Chief Seattle, "Man did not weave the web of life; he is merely a strand within it."

LOSING TOUCH

When people lose touch with their relatives, when they become isolated and disconnected from the world and the sacred dance of the year, they get lonely for those things. They hurt deep inside, and when people hurt deep inside, they lose touch with themselves. They become empty within, and illness comes into the emptiness and hides there.

19th-century illustration of a shaman in a ceremonial wolf skin.

Shamans have a deep sense of connection with their relations in the natural world.

20

SACRED ETHICS

BECAUSE ALL THINGS ARE ALIVE, ALL THINGS MUST BE RESPECTED. THE ETHICS OF SHAMANISM IS THEREFORE OF PRIME IMPORTANCE. THE FIRST STEP ON THE SHAMANIC PATH IS TO LEARN THAT EVERY ACTION MUST BE PERFORMED WITH RESPECT AND GRATITUDE. YOU CANNOT SIMPLY GO OUT AND CUT DOWN A TREE; THE TREE IS A BEING JUST AS YOU ARE. YOU NEED TO TALK TO IT, AND THANK IT FOR ITS GIFTS. YOU MUST SAY PRAYERS FOR ITS SPIRIT, AND GIVE A GIFT IN EXCHANGE FOR WHAT YOU TAKE.

DESECRATION

The recent growth in demand for quartz crystals as healing objects resulted in some highly unsacred methods of mining, such as dynamiting the crystals out of the ground—a dreadful defilement in the eyes of a traditional animist. The taking of oil from the ground can arouse similar horror, as in the case of the U'wa people of Colombia, who threatened mass suicide in the face of an oil company's plan to drill on their sacred land.

GIVING THANKS

The offering of a small token or sacred gift in return for what you take is a key feature of animistic and shamanic spirituality. When you visit a sacred place or perform a ceremony on the land, when you remove a piece of wood or take home a feather, you should always leave behind a gift.

Life is precious, and we need to take from other beings in order to live, but one day we will die and will ourselves become food; it is the nature of things. So we are grateful for the time we have, and use the things we use with gratitude. We do not take more than we need, and we always say thank you to our relatives.

Modern practices such as logging do not respect nature.
If you wish to take wood from a tree, always do so
reverently and leave a gift of thanks in exchange.

THE USES OF SHAMANISM

Some people believe that the shamans of a tribe keep the people in fear, and use their position to exercise power over others. This can happen, but it is not generally true. The shamanic path is a quest for power over ourselves and the enemies within us rather than a desire to dominate others. Following a shamanic path should provide a person with the resources to live more like a complete human being. It is important not to hide behind the glamour and mystery of shamanism. It must be a genuine spiritual search, not an ego trip to make you feel like a more interesting person.

There are many shamanic peoples who believe that their traditional teachings are for the benefit of all humanity. There are many who do not. Some traditionalists regard modern society's interest in shamanism as cultural theft. It is important to respect the view of such people, and to be careful and sincere in what you do.

There are also followers of shamanism who gather a little knowledge and regard themselves as experts. Sometimes what they do is merely disrespectful; at other times, it is dangerous. Do not hesitate to walk away if you do not like what is happening. As you learn the ways of shamanism, you will acquire a feeling for what is right. You will gain a sense of the ethics you need to follow, and part of that is acquiring the humility to acknowledge your inadequacy to a spirit or a person, and to ask for the help you need.

Tobacco, biscuits, and chocolate are just a few of the token gifts that you can offer as thanks to the spirits.

SACRED GIFTS

● Sacred gifts vary greatly, according to the culture. A small offering of tobacco is traditional for many Native Americans.

● In parts of Europe, milk, beer, or small cakes are left.

● Gold, turquoise, jade, flowers, and maize flour form part of an elaborate system of gifts appropriate to sacred places in Central America.

● Many cultures make an offering of light by lighting a candle.

We are just two-legged creatures who walk upon the earth for a short time. We are relatively small in the scheme of things, and we need to say thank you to the great powers around us. A Tibetan tribe lays out gifts of food and drink at a sky burial ceremony (above left and left); gifts left for the spirits by a Mongolian shaman (above right).

25

THE HOOP OF CREATION

STAND IN AN OPEN PLACE WHERE YOU CAN SEE A LONG WAY, AND YOU WILL NOTICE THAT YOU ARE IN THE CENTER OF A CIRCLE, THE CIRCLE OF THE HORIZON. YOUR PLACE AT THE CENTER OF THIS CIRCLE IS THE SACRED CENTER OF THE WORLD, AND THE SACRED HOOP OF THE HORIZON GOES ALL AROUND YOU. WE ARE ALL OF US, ALL OF THE TIME, IN THE SACRED CENTER OF THE WORLD, BUT WE USUALLY SIMPLY FAIL TO NOTICE IT.

All things form part of the sacred circle—the seasons of the year, the life of people and animals, and our beautiful planet.

THE SACRED CIRCLE

Native peoples all over the world have held the circle sacred for thousands of years. It is sacred because it occurs all around us:

- The sun and moon are circles.
- The stars circle the heavens.
- The year follows a circle from winter through summer and back to winter again.
- Birds make their nests in a circle.
- The power of the whirlwind is a circle.
- Trees have a roughly circular shape.
- Raindrops are round; the rainbow is a curving part-circle.
- Tribal people often build houses in circular shapes; ceremonial spaces, such as the ancient European stone circles, and Native American kivas and Sun Dance grounds, are round.

The Circle and the Cross

As you stand in the sacred center, there is always a
direction in front of you, one behind you, and one each to
left and right. There is also the sky above you, and the ground
below. The sacred circle is intersected by these points, and you can
picture yourself standing in the center of a cross whose arms stretch
out to touch the curve of the circle around you.

The sun rises in the East, and sets in the West. These directions,
therefore, form two arms of the cross—fixed points that all beings
have in common. With these in place, the other arms of the cross,
the North and South, can also be fixed. The circle and cross
become a means of making sense of the world, and together
they form the shape of the "medicine wheel."

MEDICINE IN A SHAMANIC SENSE REFERS NOT ONLY TO A MEANS OF HEALING, BUT ALSO TO THE KNOWLEDGE AND POWER INHERENT IN EVERY LIFE FORM. THE MEDICINE WHEEL IS A WAY OF GAINING ACCESS TO THE ESSENCE OF EXISTENCE. THE CIRCLE AND CROSS OF THE MEDICINE WHEEL—ALSO KNOWN AS THE "FOUR QUARTERS OF THE WORLD"—IS A SYMBOL FOUND IN MANY CULTURES ALL OVER THE GLOBE.

An ancient stone medicine wheel in North America.

The medicine wheel can enhance physical, mental, emotional, and spiritual understanding. It can also act as a guide in every area of life. Each sector of the wheel is associated with particular elements and aspects of life, although the positioning of these may vary among the many medicine wheel traditions.

THE EAST AND WEST

The rising of the sun in the East signals the birth of a new day, so the East can be regarded as the place of birth. Every new action is like a birth; every action

*We all give birth
to new life and
new actions at
each moment in
our lives. Life is
forever pregnant
with possibilities.*

comes from somewhere, happens, and
is over, making room for the next.
The sun rises and brings its heat;
the sun is fire, so fire can belong
in the East of the circle.

The West is the direction
of the setting sun, bringing
at the end of each day the
darkness of night. The sun
dies just as humans do, so
the West can be regarded as
the place of death. It is the

29

*The stone people give
shape to the world
in which we live.*

body that dies, so the West can also be home to the physical
part of our being. The East, therefore, becomes the place
of the nonphysical: spirit, action, and passion. And since
human people are able to function in ways that animal
people cannot—to build and create, and act in a spirited
way—humans can be located in the East.

The sun dies in the West each evening, only to return with
new life in the East the next day. It is in the West that the new
day makes itself ready to appear, so the West can be seen as
a place of waiting and of preparing to act at the right time.
It is a place of pregnancy and gestation. Pregnancy is the most female of times, so the
West can be the place of the female. The East, therefore, becomes the place of the male.

Every person has a mother and a father, but creation also has
a male and female side, and we are grandchildren of the sun and
the earth. If the East is the place of maleness, it must also be the
home of our Grandparent Sun, and our Grandparent Earth must
belong to the female West. The earth is the home of the stone
people, so they also belong in the West.

*The beauty of the
plant people is like
the beauty of our
emotions when they
are allowed to flower.*

Sunrise is a time of bright light, so the East is the color yellow.
The West is the home of sunset and night, so its color is black.

THE NORTH AND SOUTH

Observation of the way the world works can help to map out the
North and South of the wheel also. In the Northern Hemisphere,
the sun travels toward the West each day by swinging in a curve
over the South. South-facing areas that catch the sun are often the
places where plants grow best, so plants can be placed in the South.

Plants need water to live, just as we all do. Along with fire and
earth, it is essential to our world. Because plants are in the South,

Our minds can achieve the nobility of the animal people when we stand in balance with them.

water can be placed there also. Plants are the living beings upon which others rely. Animals eat plants, and without plants, life would not exist. Plants are mostly green, but the lifeblood of the people and animals who eat them is red, so the South can be either green or red. North-facing slopes are cool, and in winter the cold North winds bring snow. Ice lingers on the North side of trees and rocks, so the color of the North can be white.

Plant people and human people have another relative, the animal people, who, like all of us, need air to breathe. Water, fire, and earth have their place on the wheel, so we can place air, and with it the animal people, in the North.

The basic medicine wheel, therefore, comprises the four elements—fire, water, earth, and air—and the four races of the world—the plant people, the stone people, the animal people, and the human people—and each direction has a color—yellow, red (or green), black, and white.

DEPTHS OF UNDERSTANDING

See yourself standing at the sacred center of this wheel, and remember the story of the Great-Grandparents who made the sun and the earth, the beings who go on for all time, unlike plants, or animals, or people, or even mountains, who all live and die. Picture these two great beings and their sacred marriage in the center of all things, and know that this sacred marriage goes on for all time, renewing the world at each instant.

Now, as you observe the world, you can add to the wheel and gain a deeper understanding

Human beings hold onto our intent as we make our way through the world.

Sometimes we lose our balance by relying solely on our thoughts to find solutions to problems.

of the way things are. You can look at people and see that they are also medicine wheels. A person's physical body is in the earthy West, and his or her spirit is in the fiery East. Think about the water and air on the medicine wheel, and consider which part of you is your watery part and which is your airy one.

Powerful emotions can make people weep with grief or tremble with fear. Feelings can become frozen like ice, and may need to be thawed, so feelings can belong in the place of the South. Thoughts can tumble and roam like the wind, and so they can inhabit the place of air, in the North.

YOUR ETERNAL SELF

Just as the medicine wheel has a center, you too have a center, which is your true identity. We know that we are not our body, which

Children have not yet learned to freeze the water of their feelings. Their emotions flow as life touches them.

changes, ages, and dies. We are not our thoughts and feelings, because they also change over time. We are not our passionate spirit either. We have an eternal part—our soul—which is the deep, true person that sits in the center of our wheel.

The soul is not to be confused with the spirit, whose home is in the East. The spirit is the personality, action, and passion. It enables us to give birth to things, but what we generate changes and eventually dies to make room for the next thing to be born. The soul is different; it goes on, unending.

Each compass direction is associated with a color: yellow for the East, red or green for the South, black for the West, and white for the North.

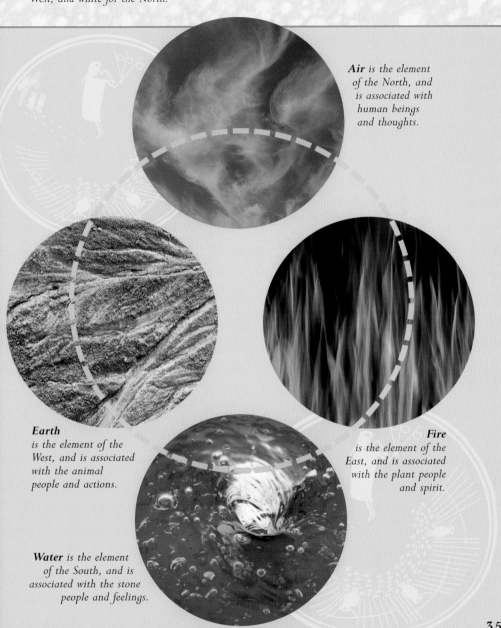

Air *is the element of the North, and is associated with human beings and thoughts.*

Earth
is the element of the West, and is associated with the animal people and actions.

Fire
is the element of the East, and is associated with the plant people and spirit.

Water *is the element of the South, and is associated with the stone people and feelings.*

MAKING A MEDICINE WHEEL

THE SYMBOLIC CIRCLES MADE IN MANY CULTURES ACT AS REMINDERS OF THE SACRED CIRCLE THAT ENCOMPASSES US ALL. THEY INCLUDE HUGE STONE CIRCLES, SUCH AS STONEHENGE IN ENGLAND, MEDICINE WHEELS, SUCH AS THE BIG HORN WHEEL IN THE UNITED STATES, THE SUN DANCE GROUNDS BUILT BY NATIVE AMERICANS SUCH AS THE LAKOTA AND CROW, AND THE INTRICATE MANDALAS MADE FROM CRUSHED CHALK AND STONE BY BUDDHIST MONKS IN TIBET. IT IS EASY TO MAKE A MEDICINE WHEEL FROM A WOODEN HOOP, AS YOUR OWN REMINDER OF THE SACRED CIRCLE.

YOU WILL NEED
- Two flexible twigs without side shoots (such as willow, ash, or hazel)
- Sharp scissors and craft knife
- Strong thread
- Soft thin leather
- Feathers, fur, and beads (optional)

1 Find two slender twigs, each 10–20 inches (25–50 cm) long, on a living tree. Ask the tree's permission to cut the wood, and leave a small gift in exchange for its gift.

2 Carefully bend one of the twigs into a tight circle, and bind the two ends firmly together with thread.

3 Wet a long thin strip of leather and wind it around the entire hoop, leaving about 5–10 inches (12–20 cm) hanging at the beginning.

4 When you come back to your beginning piece, tie the two ends of the strip together, and leave them hanging as a pair of tassels.

5 Cut the remaining twig in half and bind the two pieces into a cross shape with thread. Insert them inside the hoop to form the cross of the four directions. Trim the ends of the wood to fit, as necessary, and bind the cross into place with thread.

6 Add decorations, such as feathers, fur, and beads. Whether fancy or plain, this will be a sacred circle, mirroring your place on the sacred hoop.

Use a flexible wood such as willow, ash, or hazel to make a medicine wheel.

WORKING WITH THE MEDICINE WHEEL

A MEDICINE WHEEL IS NOT JUST A SYMBOL OF THE SACRED. IT IS A SACRED PLACE IN ITS OWN RIGHT, AND CAN BE USED AS AN ALTAR FOR YOUR OWN SACRED WORK. A MEDICINE WHEEL FOR THIS PURPOSE IS BEST MADE FROM STONES. A SIMPLE CIRCLE OF STONES—ONE FOR EACH OF THE FOUR COMPASS DIRECTIONS—IS SUFFICIENT, THOUGH YOU CAN ADD MORE AROUND THE CIRCUMFERENCE IF YOU WISH.

1 Find four stones, and talk to them, telling them why you want them. Leave a gift, and arrange the stones in a circle marking the four directions.

2 Now you can use the wheel to reflect things about your life. For example, you have a problem with a friend at work. Sit by the south stone, and ask yourself, "What do I feel about this problem?" Notice what comes into your awareness, what emotions you have, and what physical sensations you experience. Write them on a piece of paper, if that helps.

3 When you feel you have obtained a good sense of this south place, move around clockwise to the North. In this place, ask yourself, "What are the facts of the situation?" Facts do not have feelings, so try to keep emotions out of your exploration. If this proves difficult, return to the south place, and move on only when you feel sufficiently free of your feelings to do so.

4 When the facts of the situation are fairly clear, move clockwise again, all the way around the circle to the West. The West is the place of gestation; here you can sit and dream about what you need to do to solve the problem. You know what you feel; you know the facts. Here you can acquire an intuitive sense of what the problem needs, as you allow a solution to emerge.

5 Once you are clear about your course of action, move around clockwise to the East, and begin to act from the place of fire and action.

JUST AS YOU ARE IN THE CENTER OF A CIRCLE WITH THE FOUR DIRECTIONS ALL AROUND YOU, YOU ALSO HAVE THE SKY ABOVE YOU AND THE EARTH BENEATH YOU. HUMANS INHABIT A MIDDLE AREA BETWEEN THE UPPER AND LOWER WORLDS.

This ancient shamanic view of three worlds, stacked on top of one another, is echoed in many cultures. Our tradition of heaven, earth, and hell, in descending layers, is one example. Shamanism, however, does not regard heaven as a paradise, and the underworld as a place of torment; the three shamanic worlds are regions to which the shaman travels.

THE WORLD TREE

The three worlds are often said to be connected by a tree, known as the World Tree. In Norse mythology, the ash tree Yggdrasil is the tree that stands at the center of the world, and other worlds can be reached by traveling up and down its trunk. The World Tree is also a part of Native American tradition. In the Sun Dance, for example, it is the tree in the center of the sacred circle toward which all the dancers move.

The Lakota holy man Nicholas Black Elk, made famous in the book *Black Elk Speaks* by John Neihardt, tells of a vision, in which he was:

"... standing on the highest mountain of them all, and around about beneath me was the whole hoop of the world ... I saw that the Sacred Hoop of my people was one of many hoops, that made one circle ... And in the center grew one mighty flowering tree to shelter all the children of one mother and one father. And I saw that it was holy."

As we travel through this middle world of life, the sky is always above us and the ground is always beneath us.

WALKING THE WORLDS

THE MAIN WORK OF THE SHAMAN IS TO TRAVEL BETWEEN THE THREE WORLDS
TO SEEK ENLIGHTENMENT ON BEHALF OF HIS OR HER PEOPLE. SHAMANS TRAVEL TO
FIND HEALING FOR SOMEONE, OR TO FIND A PERSON, OBJECT, OR INFORMATION,
OR TO BATTLE HOSTILE SPIRITS.

These can be the spirits of illness, which need to be dealt with just as much as the physical
symptoms do. There are cultures in which shamans fight among themselves, and then a
shaman may send illness spirits to cause disharmony in people. The people fall ill, and
seek out other shamans to help them recover. This is certainly not an aspect of all
shamanic cultures—but it happens.

The shaman may also travel between the three worlds to find a person or object that is
lost in the physical world, or to seek information from the spirits, such as the whereabouts
of animals that the people need to hunt for their livelihood.

*The drum opens the gate to the spirit world
through which the shaman travels.*

ENTERING OTHER WORLDS

The shaman often enters the other worlds
by means of a drum- and song-induced
trance, but in many parts of Siberia,
Mongolia, and the Americas, psychoactive
plants serve this purpose. Some
anthropologists consider that this use of
mind-altering plants is an essential aspect
of the authentic shamanic tradition.

The use of these plants is a sacred
tradition, not a "trip" taken for pleasure.
In fact, many of the plants—such as the
peyote cactus and the South American vine

*Some shamans use sacred plants, such
as the peyote cactus, to help them
travel to the other sacred worlds.*

used to make the drink ayahuasca—have unpleasant side effects, including vomiting and diarrhea. The plants are taken as spiritual aids, and the spirit of the plant is highly respected.

THE LOWER WORLD

Some shamans travel only to the lower world, and some travel only to the upper world. The choice depends upon the individual and upon the tradition being followed. A shaman journeying to the lower world may slip down the trunk of the World Tree, and travel along its roots. In some traditions, the shaman's spirit enters the lower world through a sacred tunnel or other opening. Inside the tunnel, the shaman falls, like Alice, all the way down to the lower world.

Brimstone and pits of fire, inhabited by demons who torture the souls of the damned, are a long way from the underworld of shamanic cultures. To most shamans, the underworld is a landscape of light and form, inhabited by animals, and similar in many ways to this world. There are variations that reflect local conditions; marine peoples, such as the Inuit of Arctic North America, for example, sometimes perceive the lower world as an other-dimensional ocean deep.

TOTEM ANIMALS To the shaman, the lower world is the place of the power animals. Power animals, or totem animals, are spirits who do not manifest themselves in a physical body. They dwell in this spirit realm, and the shaman visits them to seek information, and to enlist them as personal helpers. The spirit

A shield can act as a sacred filter, blocking out reality for the journey to other worlds.

Medieval artists, such as Fra Angelico, depicted the underworld as a place of torment, a far cry from the shaman's underworld of light.

In some traditions, shamans are said to "shape shift" into animals such as wolves when journeying to other worlds.

animals aid the shamans when they journey and heal, adding their own expertise to the shamans' own. A shaman often has more than one spirit animal helper, and can have a very close relationship with the spirit animal in the lower world, and with its corresponding animal in this world.

A shaman may climb a rainbow to enter the upper world in order to ask the spirits for information.

THE SOUL AFTER DEATH Some shamanic cultures believe that deep within the lower world is the land of the dead. It is here that part of a person's soul goes after death. Many shamanists see the soul as comprising several distinct parts, each with a different destination after the body's death. Some parts stay on this earth and communicate with the family or tribe; they can be regarded as the ancestral spirit. Another part goes to the land of the dead. Yet another is reincarnated in another body.

Sometimes shamans travel in the land of the dead to find souls of the living who wandered or were taken there. This is part of the shamans' healing work; they capture or negotiate with the soul they came to find, and bring it back to this world, to reunite it with the living person and make that person whole.

THE UPPER WORLD

Shamans who go to the upper world may climb a rainbow into the sky, rise up in a cloud of smoke, or be carried on the back of a giant bird. Sometimes the shaman "shape shifts" into an animal, and the shaman's spirit becomes the animal for the duration of the journey. Shape shifting is a familiar theme in folk tales, such as the story of the werewolf,

and in shamanic cultures there are many stories of travelers encountering the local shaman in animal form.

MOON POWER The upper world of the shaman is sometimes seen as a cloudscape, and other times as a series of levels. In some cultures, the number of heavens is seven, an idea reflected in our expression of "being in seventh heaven." The shaman may also travel to the stars or the planets.

The moon, stars, and planets are associated with the upper world of the spirits.

When dancers who formed part of the Native American shamanic ghost dance movement of the late 19th century went into a trance, they were often said to "go to the moon." Sometimes they returned from their trance clutching small pieces of rock, which they swore were given to them by their ancestors who lived on the moon, as proof of their journey there.

A shaman generally travels to the upper world to seek information from the powers—the spirits of the upper world. It is here also that the shaman can receive teachings, such as how to perform a particular kind of healing.

THE MIDDLE WORLD

Although we live between the shamanic lower and upper worlds, we do not live in the shamanic middle world. This is a parallel spirit world, a shadow version of our own. The shaman travels there to find lost people or things, or to spy on other tribes' activities in time of war.

Shamans travel in the middle world when they wish to work with the spirit of the land, or the spirit of a feature of the land, such as a mountain. This is where the shaman goes to make contact with the spirit of other elements of this physical world, such as the spirit of a drum or a building. All things in this world have spirits, so all can be encountered in the middle world.

THE SACRED JOURNEY

THE JOURNEY BETWEEN THE THREE WORLDS IS THE SHAMAN'S PRIME FUNCTION. BEFORE ANY CEREMONY CAN TAKE PLACE, THEY PREPARE THEMSELVES FOR THE JOURNEY IN A RITUAL MANNER, OFTEN HELPED BY ASSISTANTS.

MAKING SMUDGE First, the shaman and all of the items to be used in the ceremony are cleansed with the sweet-smelling smoke of burning herbs. Making smoke, or "smudge," is a widespread practice, and the plants used vary according to the local environment. In northern countries, such as Siberia, cedar or juniper is often burned. In North America, the usual choice is sage leaves—either from true sage (*Salvia*), or from sagebrush, which is a member of the *Artemisia* family.

A CEREMONIAL COSTUME Ceremonies vary according to cultural tradition, and to instructions received from the spirits. In some traditions, the shaman dons a special costume or a mask.

A SACRED PLACE The shaman may also prepare a special place from which to undertake the journey. This could be an area set apart from others, which is strewn with sacred herbs or has sacred objects suspended around it.

SONGS AND AN ALTAR Shamans often sing to the spirits, using songs that they learned from the spirits or from shaman predecessors. Some traditions call for the building of a special altar to create a sacred focus for the ceremony.

THE SOUL LEAVES THE BODY As the drum beats, the shaman goes into a trance. In this state, the shaman's soul leaves his or her body and travels into the other worlds.

TALKING WITH THE SPIRITS During their journey, shamans meet and talk to sacred beings from whom they receive information. The spirits may help the shaman find a lost soul, or reveal the location of a desired object. They may provide the instructions for a new ceremony that the people must enact, or a magical item that they must make.

The planet earth viewed from space is a magnificent sight. Embark on your own sacred journey between the lower, middle, and upper worlds of the shaman to commune with the earth's spirits.

ENACTING THE JOURNEY During the journey the shaman may lie prone or dance in a trance state, and act out all the events of the journey.

BACK TO THE BODY Once the desired answers are received, the shaman thanks the spirits and returns to his or her body. The drums stop, and the ceremony is over. The shaman tells people what has happened, puts away the sacred objects, and becomes a mere person once more.

CHAPTER TWO

THE TOOLS
OF THE
Shaman

The shaman's bag of tools contains a fantastic array of magical items, some prescribed by the culture, and some derived from the shaman's personal vision and from dialogue with the spirit powers.

The tools are all made from natural local materials, such as stones, plants, and animal parts. A shaman is an artist who sculpts the wonders of the natural world into other-worldly magical art, drawing out the unseen essence of things, and working directly with their spirit. The shaman's studio is full of treasures: feathers, bones, dried animal skin and pelts, aromatic herbs, metals—curious and wonderful gifts from the abundance that is all around, each object taken and kept with reverence. The poetry of magic is made manifest in shamanic art, and with it the shamans open doorways to other worlds, through which they and the spirits travel.

THE ROLE OF SHAMANIC TOOLS

SPIRIT AND MATTER, LIKE MALE AND FEMALE, LIGHT AND DARK, GOOD AND EVIL, HOT AND COLD, ARE FUNDAMENTAL OPPOSITES. SEEMINGLY IRRECONCILABLE, THEY CONSTITUTE THE SACRED MARRIAGE AT THE CENTER OF THE MEDICINE WHEEL, AND ENERGIZE THE GREAT DANCE OF THE COSMOS IN WHICH WE ALL PARTICIPATE.

FORM AND SPIRIT

We are physical beings, living in a world of things that we can touch, and our experience of their form makes them real to us. The shaman's tools serve to marry the world of form with the world of spirit. On one level, a drum is simply a shape made from wood and animal skin; on another, it is a vehicle for wonderment. The shaman uses the drum because it is intrinsically physical and therefore a link with human physicality. Although it is possible to practice shamanism without physical objects, the combining of matter with spirit gives the ceremony energy.

FIXED INTENT

The energy present in magic is known as "intent." It is the focus of people's hearts, bodies, minds, and wills as they meet the mind, heart, and will of the spirits. Form is incomplete without spirit, and spirit is incomplete without form. When they meet, both terminals of the cosmic battery are connected, and the power flows. Tools help the shamans to fix their intent on the ceremony. In addition, the intent of all those who used the same type of tool or performed the same ceremony in the past combines to generate a powerhouse of spiritual energy.

Animal bones, skins, and feathers can all be used to make shamanic tools.

Beating on his sacred drum, a Mongolian shaman summons the power helpers of the spirit world to him.

MEDICINE POWER

A SHAMAN'S TOOLS ARE MADE FROM NATURAL MATERIALS, AND ARE THEREFORE PARTS OF BEINGS THAT HAVE SPIRITS. THIS ADDS ANOTHER DIMENSION TO THE INTENT BEHIND THE TOOL. FOR EXAMPLE, IF A SHAMAN WORKS WITH A PARTICULAR ANIMAL HELPER, SUCH AS A BEAR, USING PARTS OF AN ACTUAL BEAR BRINGS THE SPIRIT OF THE BEAR INTO THE SHAMAN'S WORK.

MEDICINE QUALITIES

Each material that is used to make a shamanic tool has a special power, known to Native Americans as a "medicine." This does not mean that the material is necessarily associated with healing, but refers to the material's inner qualities. That is why people are given "medicine names" that describe instead of label them. The name Sally Smith, for example, is an identity tag. It does not say anything about its owner, unless she is both a metal worker (smith) and a royal person (Sally, from sara, Hebrew for princess). A name such as Shadow Wolf, on the other hand, could denote someone with the qualities of both wolves and shadows. One should not adopt such a name because it sounds romantic; unless the name describes its bearer, it remains as much a label as Sally Smith is.

SACRED ATTRIBUTES

Everything in the world has a medicine: an inner quality. When you bring this medicine into the things you make, you create a more potent sacred object. Shamanic tools are richly imbued with meaning and symbolism. For example, the eagle is a powerful bird, associated with clear sight, high flying, and spirit. Many regard it as a sacred bird, and because it soars out of the range of human eyes, it is believed to be able to enter the world above. For tens of thousands of years, these medicine qualities have been associated with the eagle, so that when a shaman uses an eagle feather or a piece of eagle bone, it is a conscious connection with the bird's sacred attributes.

Modern names, such as John Smith, are merely labels. Native Americans use "medicine names" that describe their spiritual attributes. Names associated with the eagle are particularly potent.

PERSONAL POWER
AND VISION

EVERYONE IS DIFFERENT, SO IT IS IMPORTANT FOR THE SHAMAN TO DEVELOP A SENSE OF HIS OR HER OWN SPECIAL MEDICINE. THIS SENSE EMERGES GRADUALLY, AND CANNOT BE RUSHED. THE SHAMAN MUST MATURE NATURALLY OVER TIME TO GROW STRONG, LIKE A WELL-SEASONED PIECE OF WOOD. BUT THERE ARE WAYS FOR THE SHAMAN TO ENCOURAGE THIS MATURING PROCESS, AND TO LET THE SPIRITS KNOW THAT HE OR SHE IS READY TO LEARN.

19th-century engraving of a Siberian shaman dancing and singing her way into trance.

Shamans need time by themselves in this world—time for reflection and meditation, time when the shaman is open and ready to learn from the voices in the wind, the water, and the hill. In animistic spirituality, everything is alive, everything has a spirit, and everything is ready to speak to you. Some shamanic cultures regard the stone or fire as the first shaman, the original teacher of the tradition. The world and the spirits teach shamans much of what they need to know, and they must always be aware of what is happening around them.

INITIATION AND REVELATION

Shamans perform ceremony to gain initiation and knowledge. They remove themselves from society and go into the wild places, where the voices of the spirits are stronger. In Greenland, traditional shamans, known as the Angákoq, went to the most remote, barren places, where they rubbed together special spirit-calling stones for several days without stopping. These locations became places of initiation, where shamans expect the spirits to come to them and teach them. In other cultures, shamans use vision quests or fasts to contact the spirits. During the shamans' journeys, the spirits tell them which tools to make and where to obtain the materials.

Indonesian shaman in a deep trance during a ceremony.

THE **SHAMAN'S DRUM**

A SHAMAN'S DRUM IS A "HORSE," ON WHICH THE SHAMAN RIDES TO THE OTHER WORLDS, CARRIED BY ITS SOUND. THAT IS HOW SOME TRADITIONAL SIBERIAN SHAMANS DESCRIBE THEIR DRUMS. THE DRUM IS THE MOST COMMONLY FOUND SACRED OBJECT IN SHAMANIC CULTURES ALL OVER THE WORLD. MADE FROM RAW ANIMAL SKIN STRETCHED ACROSS A WOODEN HOOP, THE DRUM'S VOICE THUNDERS OUT AS THE SHAMANIC CEREMONY BEGINS.

NATURAL WOOD AND SKIN

Most shamans' drums are of the kind known as "frame drums"—a skin pulled tightly across a wooden frame. Often, the skin covers one side only, but some drums have two skins, one on each side. The drum is made in a sacred way. Often shamans experience a dream or a vision, instructing them in the construction of the drum. They may be told which animal skin to choose, and which wood; they may even be shown the tree from which the wood must be cut. This is often the tree that is associated with the World Tree, so the drum is likely to be made of birch or ash. By using the wood of the World Tree, the shaman identifies with it and combines its medicine in the drum. Since the shaman uses the drum to travel up and down the World Tree to the other worlds, the drum's wood assists the journey.

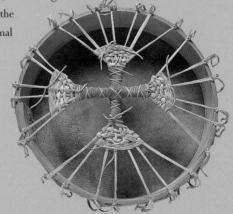

The drum is the horse on which a shaman rides in ecstasy to the other worlds. It is made from raw animal skin stretched tightly across a wooden hoop frame.

*The skins of shamanic drums are often painted
with a map of the three worlds, or images of
the shaman's animal spirit helper.*

The skin of the drum is normally of deer or elk, but sometimes of horse or another animal. The animal's hair or fur is usually removed, but otherwise, the skin remains natural. Leather cannot be used because of the chemical changes it undergoes during softening. Drum skin is hard, raw hide; the skin is taken from the animal, cleaned, dehaired, and stretched on the frame.

MAGICAL SYMBOLISM

The drum can be plain or highly decorated. The decorations all have medicine meaning to the shaman. The skin may be painted with a map of the three worlds for navigation during the shaman's journeys. Sometimes the designs are of animals, usually the shaman's helpers, or the animal most deeply associated with the people. In a hunting society, for example, the drum may bear representations of the prey, so that the shaman can both identify with it and locate it in the spirit world.

Single-sided drums are generally held by means of a handle at the back. This is usually in the center of the drum, to keep the correct balance. The handle is often rich in symbolism. It is sometimes carved in the shape of a person—either the shaman, the spirit of the drum, or the shaman's spirit helper. The handle is frequently cross-shaped, representing the cross of the four directions. Many drums have magical objects hung from the back: bells, small leather bags containing charms, models of animals, and sometimes weapons that the shaman may need on journeys. The drums are often equipped with little pieces of wood or metal that vibrate against the skin when it is beaten. These produce a buzzing, rasping sound while the drum is played, somewhat like a snare on a snare drum.

BLESSING THE DRUM

When a drum is made, it is blessed and "awakened." This is a ceremony of dedication to the spirit of the drum. The drum may be rubbed in animal fat, blood, or milk. Beer, vodka, whisky, or perfume may be poured or spat over it as a blessing. Prayers are said about it, and it is smudged in sweet smoke. After this ceremony, it is no longer an object of wood and skin; it is magical and holds great power.

THE SHAMAN'S RATTLE

THE SECOND MOST IMPORTANT TOOL FOR MANY SHAMANS IS THE RATTLE. IN MONGOLIA AND SIBERIA, SHAMANS OFTEN USE A DRUMSTICK THAT IS ALSO A RATTLE. DURING THE PERIOD OF SHAMANIST OPPRESSION IN THE FORMER SOVIET UNION, WHEN MANY DRUMS WERE SEIZED AND BURNED, SHAMANS FREQUENTLY CONTINUED TO PRACTICE WITH JUST THE RATTLING DRUMSTICK.

MAKING A RATTLE

The function of rattles is similar to that of drums. Shamans journey with them, call to the spirits with them, and use them for healing. Many rattles are made from the same materials as drums: skin and wood. Thick rawhide is dampened and formed into a small balloon shape, which dries stiff and hard to become the rattle head. The head is filled with stones, and a wooden handle is pushed into the opening and attached. Rattles are also made from the dried gourds of plants, and from turtle shells, animal horns, seedpods, metal, and carved wood.

FILLING A RATTLE

The filling of a rattle is a sacred affair. The materials vary but normally include sacred or special stones. In North America, some tribal nations use the tiny quartz rocks that ants bring out of their nests. These are considered very sacred, and a specific number of them are put into the rattle. This number has a symbolic meaning. The Lakota, for example, have a tradition of 405 spirit helpers, so 405 ant rocks are put into a rattle to celebrate and communicate with these helpers.

Rattles may be painted or have charms tied to them. Some are hung with bells or feathers and animal hair. They become a sacred shamanic tool, and may be passed on after their owner's death to another shaman, accumulating sacredness and power as they pass through the generations.

The shaman uses the rattle to sing power songs, and to diagnose and treat those who are ill.

SHAMANIC HEALING

IN SHAMANIC CULTURES, SICKNESS IS A SPIRITUAL MATTER. ILLNESS IS THE RESULT OF
A MISALIGNMENT BETWEEN THE PERSON AND THE WORLD, OR BETWEEN THE SOUL
AND THE BODY, SO SHAMANS TREAT ILLNESS FROM A SPIRITUAL PERSPECTIVE.

*Herbal healing is practiced
in all cultures of the world.*

Shamans may use plants containing natural
chemicals—of the type also synthesized by drug
companies—but it is the spirit of the plant that
helps the shaman heal. Some shamans have a deep
relationship with one particular plant, which they use
to treat many illnesses, even those for which the plant
has no physical curative properties. Ceremony and
sacred tools are almost always used, to summon the
spirits' aid and to develop the intent of both shaman
and patient to make the healing work.

SOUL LOSS

In the shamanic view, the most frequent reason for
illness is "soul loss." Many shamanic cultures see the human soul as having a number of
parts, and believe that certain of these can be lost or removed from the main core of the
soul. The loss leaves the owner in a lethargic, depressed state—without vitality, fire, and
passion for life. The sufferer may want to sleep a great deal, and have little appetite for
food or stimuli. The person can become withdrawn, and may perceive life as a dream
from which it is impossible to awaken. He or she may feel lightheaded, or fuzzy, and
unable to act decisively.

A WESTERN EPIDEMIC

Some shamans think that soul loss is epidemic in Western societies. In their view, spiritual
starvation, isolation from the natural world, and an institutionalized powerlessness in the
face of work and social demands cause many in the Western world to lose parts of their

*Many shamans
believe that we
become spiritually
starved and lose
parts of our soul if
we are isolated from
the natural world.*

When we lose our soul, we lose a vital part of ourselves. Many shamans believe that modern drugs and stress at work can lead to soul loss.

soul in order to survive. The illnesses and the sense of isolation experienced by many in Western society are symptomatic of this, and there is a need to regain the older shamanic ways in order to establish good cultural health.

THE FLIGHT OF THE SOUL

Souls can be lost for a variety of causes. The loss can happen because of a trauma, shock, or accident. It can occur when a loved one dies and the person left behind does not want to carry on alone, or as a result of emotional, physical, or sexual abuse. Chemicals and drugs can expel the soul from the body; so can anesthetics, which some shamans see as a major shortcoming of Western medical practice. The soul, or part of it, simply wishes to flee a situation that it cannot tolerate, so it removes itself to another place. That is usually the lower world—and it is there that the shaman generally seeks it.

RECAPTURING THE SOUL

Once the soul part is found, the shaman can capture or negotiate with it, in order to return it to the body. However, the body may not have enough spiritual power to keep hold of it for long, especially if the loss had been major or long-lasting. In that case, it may be necessary to conduct ceremonial work beforehand to give the patient sufficient spiritual energy for the reconciliation.

INTRUSION

The other main cause of illness is believed to be the invasion of the victim's energy by another spirit energy—a phenomenon generally known as an intrusion. If a person is dis-spirited due to soul loss, for example, another spirit entity can enter the sufferer's body to fill the void. That is what happens in the case of possession. The invading spirit could be the spirit of an illness. Like all things in the world, sickness has a spirit, and that spirit can intrude upon the body, especially if the patient is already incomplete because of soul loss.

BROKEN RELATIONSHIPS

In shamanic societies illnesses are also often seen as resulting from a breakdown in a relationship between the person and the natural world. The sufferer may have hunted in a disrespectful manner, or encroached upon sacred land without the correct ceremonial procedures being carried out. The ensuing illness may be ascribed to an intrusion by powerful nature spirits, or their theft of the person's soul. In these cases, the shaman acts as an intermediary between the offended spirit and the sick person, reestablishing the relationship, and conducting ceremonies to restore the balance.

If we abuse the world around us, it will break down.

Energy Darts

Some cultures practice darker forms of shamanism, in which people are said to employ sorceresses to shoot magical energy darts at their enemies. These darts of energy are purported to enter the energy body of the victim, where they cause sickness, disability, and even death. The darts are regarded as a form of intrusion, and the healing shaman deals with them accordingly.

This 1,500-year-old jar from Peru shows a shaman examining a sick woman.

Sucking Medicine

The main method of dealing with an intrusion is to remove it. This is often accomplished by the technique known as "sucking medicine." Using his or her intent, the shaman sucks the intrusion out of the patient and into his or her own mouth. The intrusion is then vomited or spat out to remove it safely from the shaman's own energy body. This is a dangerous healing technique. The shamans who perform it must have perfect intent in order to rid themselves of all vestiges of the intrusion, or they could acquire the patient's disease.

THE **TOOLS** OF **HEALING**

Shamanic healing is an art in every sense of the word. It employs ritual, ceremonial, and medical knowledge, but also creative skills. Creativity is especially evident in the vision and making of the objects used in the diagnosis and treatment of disease.

Shamanic cultures throughout the world make healing objects for their shamans to use. In addition to drums and rattles, musical soundmakers include whistles, Jews' harps, bells, and even fiddles. Other healing tools are paintings and body art, masks, costumes, dolls, charms and magical fetishes, wands, sacred smoking pipes, protection bundles, spirit catchers, carved sucking tubes, and fans made from single feathers or entire bird wings. Constructions, such as altars and sacred spaces, are the equal of many a modern art installation.

USING THE SACRED TOOLS

The shaman uses the sacred tools to assess the nature of the illness, to call to the spirits, to seek out a lost soul, to remove an intrusion, to address the lack of balance between the sick person and the world, and to restore the right relationship.

DOWSING AND REMOVAL

The shaman learns to diagnose the energy body of a sick person—dowsing with a rattle or a feather, for example, to determine where the body's energy has been intruded. The intrusion is removed with a sucking tube made from bone, a hooked eagle claw, or a bunch of powerful feathers held like a hand. By means of these tools, the shaman's intent reaches deep into the patient to grab out the illness.

A Tibetan bell and two types of feather fan used for healing.

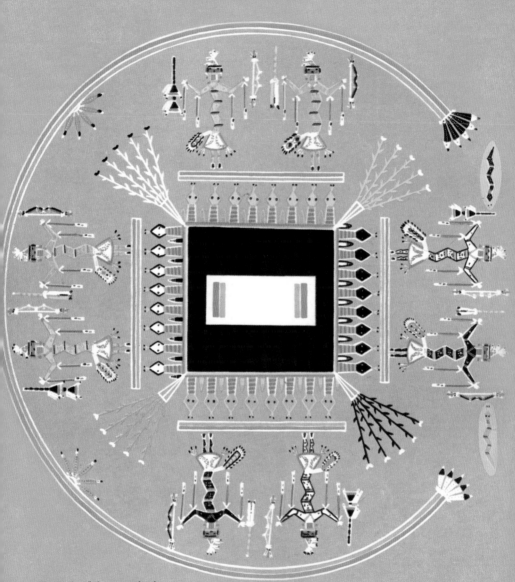

The tools of shamanic healing
often show the creative beauty
of human inventiveness, such
with this Diné sand painting.

CALLING to the SPIRITS

THE SPIRITS ARE EVERYWHERE. THE SHAMANS STAND WITHIN THIS GREAT TOTALITY OF SACRED LIFE—AND THE SPIRITS TALK TO THEM. SHAMANS USE MANY WAYS OF CONNECTING WITH THE SPIRITS.

Whatever the shamans' method, it is done with respect for the spirit Grandfathers and Grandmothers, Uncles and Aunts, whose help they seek. The spirits will hear the shamans, because their hearts are good, and their intent is set on walking between the worlds.

Some shamans use the poisonous fly agaric mushroom to induce a trance.

REACHING THE SPIRITS

Shamans can pray for aid from specific spirit helpers, such as the sacred ancestors, to whom they offer a gift of tobacco or food. They can sing ancient spirit-calling songs, or use the drum, rattle, or other instrument to entice the spirits to appear. They can offer sweet-smelling smoke to the winds, or tie flags to trees or boulders. They can perform spirit-calling ceremonies, such as the shamanic seance used by the Lakota Yuwipi. They can go without food or water and sleep for prolonged periods in an isolated place to induce vision and spiritual communication. They can dance for days on end, until the boundary of this world and the spirit world blurs. They can take psychoactive plants in tightly controlled ceremonies to shift their perception into the spirit world.

WAYS TO CALL THE SPIRITS
- Prayers and gifts.
- Ancient spirit-calling songs.
- Offering smoke to the winds.
- Tying flags to trees or boulders.
- Playing the drum, rattle, bell, or other instrument.
- Performing ceremonies, such as shamanic seances.
- Fasting and sleep deprivation, often in an isolated setting.
- Continuous dancing for long periods of time.
- Taking psychotropic plants under ritual conditions.

The spirits are all around us—in the sky and the earth, in plants and animals.

ALTARS AND SHRINES

THE WORLD OF EVERYDAY LIFE, ALTHOUGH CONNECTED TO THE SACREDNESS OF
EVERYTHING, SOMETIMES NEEDS A MORE FOCUSED SACRED SPACE. AN ALTAR OR
SHRINE—WHETHER IT IS HIGH CHURCH, BUDDHIST, OR SHAMANIC—IS JUST SUCH A
PLACE, SET APART FROM THE EVERYDAY WORLD.

HOMEMADE ALTARS

In addition to the altars used in various spiritual traditions, humans seem to have an
instinctive propensity for creating impromptu altars and shrines. The death of a famous
person is often marked by a spontaneous public altar of photos, flowers, candles, and
even stuffed animals. People frequently arrange photos and other special objects on the
mantelpiece in a ritualistic way, with flowers and sometimes candles, and probably with
no thought beyond the fact that the arrangement looks attractive.

A SACRED SPACE

In animistic cultures, altars and shrines are often reserved for the
spirits—to honor them, or to make offerings to them. They are also
used to keep ceremonial objects pure. In a place that is "not of this
world," such tools can be stored with the respect they deserve.

*All cultures share a sense
of sacred space, and all
spiritual traditions use
some form of altar.*

   In many traditions, shamans place all of their ceremonial objects
on an altar in front of them when they perform a ceremony. The
altar may be on a low table (a shamanic altar is often referred to as
a *mesa*, the Spanish for table), or on a special cloth on the floor. In
either case, it is a place that the shaman makes separate from the
everyday world. By creating a sacred space, the shamans announce
to the spirits and to the world around them that they are engaged
in a sacred activity. They proclaim that they are stepping out of the
world of the everyday into the bigger picture.

*A shamanic altar is a place "not of this world,"
where the spirits are honored. Ceremonial tools
are often kept there to retain their purity.*

INTENT, OBJECTS,
AND MAGIC

SHAMANS OFTEN SET UP ALTARS TO FOCUS THEIR INTENT ON THE PERFORMANCE OF A PARTICULAR CEREMONY OR TASK. THE ALTAR IS LIKE A SACRED MISSION STATEMENT, WRITTEN IN THE LANGUAGE OF THE SPIRITS.

HEALING AT A DISTANCE

For example, the shaman may wish to heal and protect a sick person who is far from the love and support of those who requested the ceremony. In the absence of the patient, a doll representing the person can be placed on a special altar. To generate even more intent, the doll can be dressed in the sick person's clothes or have some of the person's hair or belongings tied to it. The intention is that the doll becomes the patient, so that healing carried out on the doll is carried out on the person who needs it. This is made clear to the spirits also, so that they understand the purpose of the ceremony.

DISPELLING DANGER

If the patient is under some kind of threat, the doll may be laid on a bed of protective herbs in the center of the altar, or be wrapped in a cloth of red, the protective color. Charms that repel danger, or material with safeguarding properties, such as salt, may encircle it. Mirrors may be placed around it, facing outward to reflect away any harmful intent. In this way, positive intent combines with a magical language to speak to the spirits in clear and powerful terms.

MAGICAL OBJECTS

The intent, although attached to an altar, is the same energy that attaches to any magical object, such as a charm. In fact, a charm is a tiny portable altar. Whether it is a St. Christopher medal or a rabbit's foot, it carries a clear intent and a message to the spirit. When an object has spiritual intent, it helps the world of spirit and matter to touch—and the magic flows.

A shaman's intent can be attached to charms such as a St. Christopher medal or small doll. A shaman may use a doll to represent a sick person during a healing ceremony, surrounding it with salt and reflective mirrors to safeguard the patient and deflect harmful intent.

Medicine bundles, medicine bags, and magical charms hold the shaman's protective intent.

In shamanic cultures, such items often carry an elaborate burden of meaning. Made from sacred materials, rich in spiritual language and significance, they can become entire stories of intent rather than simple signs to spirits. They can be charms for hunting, war charms, childbirth or fertility charms, charms to safeguard the traveler, personal protection charms, charms to help in healing or divination, or charms to connect people with their animal spirit helpers.

Such charms are sometimes known as "bundles," because they often consist of many items bundled together in cloth or leather. Another name for them is "medicine bag," because they are items of medicine, or spirit, within a small bag.

MEDICINE BUNDLES

A bundle holds intent. For example, a shaman's personal medicine bag contains items that reflect its owner, and therefore remind the shaman who he or she truly is. That reminder amplifies and strengthens the shaman's intent. The bag may contain parts of the shaman, such as hair or nail clippings, to make the bundle even more a part of him or her. It may hold parts of animals that are sacred to the shaman, such as fur, feathers, or claws. There may be reminders of spirit powers with which the shaman works, such as the four colors that the shaman associates with the sacred four directions or a small medicine wheel. If the bag's owner is a hunter, it may contain miniature weapons or tiny fetishes that represent the prey. An artist may store objects that represent his or her art. The bag contains substances seen as protective, and possibly reminders of the shaman's family and people to locate its owner within his or her society.

THE SWEET GIFTS OF THE PLANT PEOPLE

GREEN—THE COLOR OF PLANTS—IS LOVED BY HUMANS THROUGHOUT THE WORLD.
PLANTS GROW ALMOST EVERYWHERE: HOT OR COLD, WET OR DRY—SOMEHOW A
PLANT WILL FIND A PLACE TO SURVIVE, AND PROBABLY THRIVE.

GIFT GIVERS

Plants are the first sacred gift givers. They give to animals, so that animals can eat them.
The animals are often hunted in turn by humans, but without the plants, there would be
no hunt. Plants also give their food directly to humans, and they give us medicines, color,
scent, fiber to make rope and cloth, and wood for tools and construction.

SMUDGE SMOKE

Shamans use plants for many purposes, but
perhaps the most immediate is to make
smudge smoke. This smoke, rising from
ornate metal containers, pottery bowls, or
simple seashells, goes out to the spirit,
touching the sacred with its beautiful scent.

Cleansing herbs are burned to dispel
unwanted spirits and residual energy.
Ceremonial places, objects and participants,
gifts, and ritual food are all "washed" in
the smoke. It prepares the place, and puts
everyone into a sacred frame of mind and
heart for the sacred activity. Other herbs
act as sweet offerings to call to the spirits.
They are generally herbs with a
sweeter smell than the tangy scents
of the cleansing herbs.

CLEANSING AND SWEET HERBS

The list of aromatic burning herbs
is almost endless. Where one herb
reaches the limit of its growing area—
perhaps due to climatic conditions—
another equally fragrant herb will
thrive and be used for smudge smoke.
These are some of the most widely
used cleansing and sweet herbs:

CLEANSING HERBS	SWEET HERBS
Sage	Tobacco
Rosemary	Woodruff
Cedar	Frankincense
Juniper	Copal
Wormwood	Sweetgrass
Lavender	Mugwort

*Shamans use cleansing herbs to dispel
unwanted energies and sweet herbs to
attract healing spirits.*

83

PSYCHOACTIVE PLANTS

SOME SHAMANIC TRADITIONS HAVE A RELATIONSHIP WITH CERTAIN PLANTS, WHICH THEY CALL UPON FOR GUIDANCE. THESE ARE PLANTS WHOSE PROPERTIES AFFECT THE CHEMISTRY OF HUMANS IN A WAY THAT ALTERS THEIR PERCEPTION OF THE WORLD.

USE AND ABUSE

The drug problem that plagues the modern world is totally removed from this respectful use of plant spirits. Modern drug users are not held within ceremony while under the drugs' effects, nor are their visions analyzed afterward. Many shamanic teachers are appalled by the modern world's disrespectful attitude toward these sacred plant teachers.

RITUAL AND ANALYSIS

The use of the plants in shamanism is ritualized by the enactment of special ceremonies. Prescribed songs are sung and the spirits are called upon for help. The dance chief or ceremony leader has great knowledge of the likely effects of the plant, and of ways to safeguard the participants. The plant users experience the teachings and visions, and are grounded once more by the dance chief. The chief encourages them to share the experience, in order to make sense of it and determine its relevance to their lives.

PSYCHOACTIVE PLANTS

- A South American vine; its bark is made into the drink ayahuasca.
- The Peyote and San Pedro cactuses; to be chewed or macerated in water.
- Mushrooms, such as psilocybin and fly agaric, are eaten.
- Berries and seeds include the seeds of the morning glory vine, mescal beans (from the Texas mountain laurel), and herbs such as diviner's sage. Seeds may be ground and soaked in water for consumption.

WARNING

Shamans do not use teacher plants for a pleasure trip. The plants are often harmful, and can cause unpleasant side effects. Some are potentially lethal; for example, less than half a mescal bean is a fatal dose for an adult. While others are less toxic, *all* are approached with extreme reverence.

Some shamanic traditions work with the sacred spirits of natural teacher plants to gain a greater depth of understanding.

CHAPTER THREE

WALKING
YOUR OWN
Path

Although it is impossible to become a
shaman by reading a book, the ways of
understanding described here can give you
much beauty and wisdom as you travel on
the "earth walk" of your life.

It is natural to imitate at first. You
will probably find yourself drawn to
a particular culture—whether Native
American, Siberian, Aboriginal, or another.
The chances are that you do not belong to
that culture (even if your biological roots
do). But it can teach you.

You cannot be a Tibetan, a Siberian, or
a Lakota; you can only be a person who is
learning to be a true human being. As you
grow in these ways, the spirits talk to you,
and what you do becomes not imitation,
but an expression of your deep personal
relationship with the sacred.

FINDING YOUR
PERSONAL VISION

SHAMANISM IS A GNOSTIC SPIRITUAL TRADITION. THAT MEANS IT IS NOT IMPOSED FROM OUTSIDE THROUGH CREED OR DOGMA; IT IS A SPIRITUALITY THAT IS DEVELOPED FROM A PERSON'S OWN KNOWLEDGE OF THE WORLD AND HIS OR HER INDIVIDUAL EXPERIENCE OF SPIRIT.

A UNIQUE PATH

You can walk only your own path—no one else's. You must learn your own strengths and weaknesses, your own language of sacredness, your own ways of asking the spirits to help and work with you. You must find the tools you need for your practice, and preferably also construct them yourself.

To have intent, the things you do must be real; they cannot be playacting. You must be ruthlessly honest about whether a ceremony is yours to perform, whether what you do comes from your heart—or from your head. Without some prior sacred knowledge, that is very difficult, which is why you need a reputable teacher. The teacher gives you a road map, shows you what to look out for and what to avoid, helps you to check that your vehicle is running smoothly, and shows you how to fix it if it goes wrong. Once you have a taste for the authentic, you will know what the journey should feel like.

Group religions impose their creed or dogma on their followers. In shamanism, you must search for your own personal vision.

YOUR SPIRITUAL MAP

Once you know the land, you will no longer need the road map. You will have your own map inside you, a map with the landmarks that are important to you: the chart of your spiritual landscape. You will develop your own shamanic ways and animistic wisdom, and you will be able to travel the landscape of world and spirit with confidence.

Wherever we walk, we can still walk in a sacred manner on the sacred earth.

TALKING TO THE SPIRITS

Shamanism is not in you like some magical power. It is not something you do from yourself, in isolation, like a superhero. It is a dialogue and a service to the spirits, so the first step is to find ways to talk to them.

THE POWER OF PRAYER

Instead of relying on an intermediary, such as a minister, to pray for you, you must invest your prayers with your own power, and pray with the authority you possess as your own priest or priestess. Shamans pray a lot. They say, "Thank you, Grandfather" when something good happens. They talk to the ancestors. They talk to the animal spirits, and to all of the other spirits with which they work. This is prayer—but a far more direct experience than the "hands together and eyes closed" that many of us learned in school.

HOW TO PRAY

Talk to the spirits each day. There is no need to make a special time for it, unless you find it helpful. The words will vary each time, because you are speaking from your heart, and not from a book of others' words.

Talk to the spirits in your own way. If you do not know what to say, tell them so. Introduce yourself by saying your name, and telling them that you are happy to be alive. Thank the Creator for the sky, whether it is gray or blue. There are always things to give thanks for: your sight, your hearing, or your sense of touch; the food you ate yesterday, or the air you breathe today.

Find your own voice, however hesitant, and use it as well as you can. Open your mouth and speak out loud. Do not let the words rattle around in your head like peas in a can; let them come out of your mouth like flowers opening in the garden.

If you hurt, then say so. Tell the spirits what hurts, and thank the spirits for the things that do not hurt. If you feel brave, thank the spirits for the hurt that is helping you to learn and letting you know that you are alive. As a Tantric Tibetan teacher said, "If you are falling from a high cliff in the mountains to your death, it is a terrible shame not to appreciate the beauty of the splendid view as you fall."

A Mongolian shaman stands in the center of a sacred circle with the spirits of life around him.

*Dramatic natural locations are often
seen as sacred, but places like your
street and garden are equally spiritual.*

A WAY TO PRAY

**Talk to the spirits every day in the way you
find best. Here is one way to pray, which
you could adapt and make your own.**

1 Begin the day by giving thanks. Go to
your table, or altar, and light a candle.
Holding a feather, raise your hand to
Grandfather Creator, and say, "Thank
you" for the blessings of the day.

*18th-century engraving of a
Siberian shaman singing and
dancing beneath a horse sacrifice.*

2 Lower your hand toward Grandmother
Earth, from whom all things come, and thank her for all you have.

3 Turn to each of the four directions, honor the powers that live at each
one, and thank them for their help.

4 Thank the spirit guardians of the land, and any particular god or
goddess associated with the place where you live.

5 Thank the animal, plant, and stone people who live on the
land with you.

6 Thank the Grandfather and Grandmother ancestors, both of the land
you live on and of the spiritual traditions you follow.

7 Be sure to say "those of you who love me" to each of the spirit powers
you call, because just like people in the street, not everything out there is
well intentioned toward you.

SMUDGING

Smudging yourself and your home every day helps you to build your intent to follow a shamanic way. Smudging herbs are easy to obtain. You can buy smudge sticks, but it is rewarding to collect your own herbs.

How to Smudge

1 Smudge your rooms by burning the herbs in a shell or a pottery bowl. Some cultures do not use shells, because they consider it disrespectful to the water; other traditions say it is good to bring the water element to the ceremony.

2 Make sure your container is sufficiently heat-proof, because the smudge can burn strongly.

3 Open a window as the smudge burns to release anything that the smudge drives out.

4 Do not blow on the smudge. Fan it with a paper fan, or a fan made from bird feathers.

5 Let the smoke travel everywhere, but be respectful of other people who might become alarmed if they smell it.

6 Fan the sweet clouds over yourself and your loved ones, allowing the smoke to surround you entirely, and washing your arms and hands in it.

Using the Herbs

It is essential to be respectful in your collection and use of smudging herbs. The quest for the sacred can become a serious threat to the environment. Sweetgrass, for example, is a reedlike plant that grows very slowly. Over the past few years, it has been overharvested in some areas, causing the loss of its natural beds.

You can smudge your home and your treasured objects on a daily basis. You can also smudge your loved ones and yourself. When you do a healing or perform a ceremony, it is also good to smudge first. Soon you will find yourself experiencing a great sense of the sacred from this act, as the old ways weave their simple magic upon you.

Wash yourself and your home in sweet smudge smoke to develop your sense of the sacred.

BEING WHOLE

BEING A WHOLE PERSON MEANS THAT YOU ARE NOT RUNNING AROUND THE EDGE OF YOUR LIFE—YOU ARE STANDING FIRMLY IN THE CENTER OF IT. THE MEDICINE WHEEL IS ALL AROUND YOU, AND WITHIN YOU. YOU HAVE YOUR EMOTIONS, YOUR BODY, YOUR MIND, AND YOUR SPIRIT, BUT YOU ARE MORE THAN THESE, BECAUSE AT THE CENTER OF THE WHEEL IS YOUR SOUL.

THE SPIRITUAL PATH

Following a righteous path will help to make you a good and law-abiding person, but following a truly spiritual path will enable you to grow. On the spiritual path, life will seek you out and bring challenges that cause you to become bigger than you are. If you read this book and think, "Hey, this stuff makes sense," it could be that you have stepped onto a spiritual path—and life will never be the same again.

LIVING ON THE EDGE

Imagine for a moment that you are a flat circle, like a medicine wheel, with the four parts of yourself—mind, body, spirit, and emotion—all around you on the edge of that circle. Now widen this to visualize everyone in the same way. Picture us all with one leg in the center of the circle, as if we were big round tables with a single central leg.

If you have a lot of emotional weight at the south of your table, your table can tip and demand much of your everyday energy to stop it from falling over. The same will be true of the north if you have mental concerns throwing that area out of balance. You could be so spiritual that you are no earthly good—making the east of your table top-heavy. Or perhaps you care too much about your physical comfort, tipping the west of your

Many people rush through life, concerned with material things, and fail to find the path to spiritual growth.

Becoming too concerned with one aspect of life—emotional, mental, spiritual, or physical—can make you lose your balance.

If you cease running around on the edge of life and find your sacred center, you will achieve balance and be able to cope with life's adversities.

table. As your personal table tilts off balance—first one way, and then another—you need to expend a lot of energy just to prevent the entire table from falling over; you run around on the edge of your life.

Spiritual traditions spotlight this running around, and help you to deal with it. They show you how to clear your table of clutter, and to make it a sacred table, or *mesa*. The more you do this, the more you move into your sacred center, and connect with your soul, and as this happens, you become more grounded and balanced. Your table's central leg can support an enormous amount of weight if the weight is in the center of your life. It is only when we run around on the edge of our life that it is such hard work.

Shamans strive to become centered in their lives.

BECOMING CENTERED

Most of us do spend the best part of our lives running around the edge, expending all of our subtle energy. So what will you do when you suddenly have more energy at your disposal?

It may sound wonderful at first, but think for a moment. We live in a world filled with people living on the edge. It makes us all the same; the sharing is comfortable. We derive drama, entertainment, and companionship from living this way. If you move out of that habit of living, your relationship with others will change. That is the price of true wholeness.

HEALING THE PAST

You are here now, which means that you survived the past. As we fall from the mountain, we must use the opportunity to admire the view, so the things that obscure our vision must be cleared away.

Shedding Your Fear

The first enemy in the line of sight is fear. Fear is the foe that stops people from moving from the past to the present. We fear because of what our experiences led us to believe about the world. We project that belief into the future, convinced that the same will happen again. We do not live in the real now; we shadowbox the imagined future.

This belief about the world is like a call that we send out. We call what we fear to come and scare us, and by so doing we make the world a more predictable and therefore seemingly safer place (even if our fears also make it unpleasant). Ceremony is one of the best methods of removing fears and hurts. It is where the spirits can join with psychotherapy to form a powerful healing union.

A Healing Ceremony
This ceremony acts to build the intent you need in order to sever your links with a hurtful past. It may need to be performed many times.

1 Ask a trusted friend to act as your anchor, witness, assistant, and bodyguard. Arm the person with an object that can act as a sword, such as a large, strong, straight feather.

2 Create a circle big enough to stand in. Make the circumference of salt or sage leaves, and cover the inside with red cloth.

3 Smudge your friend, yourself, the space, the sword, and the circle. Call aloud to the powers who love you to come and help, and to witness your healing. When this is done, step solemnly into the circle. ➤

To walk toward a free future, we need to stop carrying the fears that have shaped our past.

*Use a red cloth, a circle of sage or salt,
and a feather to perform a healing
ceremony to remove your fears.*

4 The circle is now a sacred place outside of the normal world. Standing within it, call to any people who have hurt you in the past. Let them appear, in your mind's eye, outside of your circle.

5 You can call to anyone, alive or dead. Thank them from your heart for the lessons they taught you, both pleasant and unpleasant. Thank them only as much as you are truly able—do not simply mouth the words.

6 See yourself and the people you call as dancers in the great dance of life. Try not to pass judgment on what the dance between you was like; simply see it as a dance, neither good or bad.

7 When you have said all that you need to say at this time, you must release them. See in your mind's eye a cord connecting your belly to their belly. This is the cord of intent that links you to them. It must be severed for you to move on. Your friend, standing outside of the circle, has the sword that will cut the cord.

8 Thank the spirit from your past, and say, "I release you now without blame." As you do so, your sword bearer must swing the sword down between you and the spirit, with all his or her intent to cut the cord.

9 You must now banish the spirit by saying, "Thank you, and I banish you now from this place." Say these words three times out loud.

10 Once it is done, thank the powers whom you called to help. Cleanse the sword and the room with smudge, remove the sacred circle, and carefully dispose of the salt or sage. Give your friend a gift, and then go out to the land by yourself to make your own quiet prayers of thanks and to offer the land a small gift, such as some tobacco, milk, or chocolate.

HEALING WITH THE ELEMENTS

DISEASE, AS THE WORD IMPLIES, IS A STATE IN WHICH YOU ARE NO LONGER AT EASE IN YOURSELF. THE FIRST STEP OF SHAMANIC HEALING IS THEREFORE DEVOTED TO RETRIEVING YOUR INNER HARMONY. IT IS NECESSARY TO WORK WITH THE SPIRIT AS WELL AS THE BODY, AND TO LET YOUR RELATIVES IN THE NATURAL WORLD HELP YOU.

Fire is considered to be a cleansing element in many cultures.

RELEASE THROUGH THE EARTH

If you are suffering from indigestion, ask yourself what it is in your life that you cannot digest—what you literally cannot stomach. Go out into nature, and where it is quiet, dig a hole in the ground, and lie down and talk into that hole about all the things that you feel are wrong in your life. You can yell, sob, cough, vomit, and moan into that hole, and it will take it, without judgment. When you have finished, thank the earth, fill the hole back in, and plant a seed there to turn all of the feelings you put into the hole into a growing thing.

WATER, FIRE, AND AIR

Instead of a hole, you could find a fast-flowing river—in the mountains, if possible. Lie on a bridge or a flat rock, with your head over the gushing water, and pour your heart out to the water spirit that passes below you. You can also use fire to release your pain. Build a sacred fire, while praying to the fire spirits. Then write down all your hurts on a piece of paper, smudge the paper, and give it to the fire to be burned and borne away. Or you can confide your troubles to the air. Go to a high place that has the wind blowing fast around it, and let your voice and tears and pain be carried away in the wind.

GIVING THANKS

Whichever method you choose to release your pain, do it with the understanding that the earth, the water, the fire, and the air are living beings that wish to help you. Always thank the spirits, and leave them gifts when you have finished.

The power of water can wash away the emotions you wish to be rid of.

HEALING OTHERS

SHAMANS DO FAR MORE THAN ADVISE SICK PEOPLE HOW TO FIND A CURE; THEY PRACTICE NUMEROUS METHODS OF DIAGNOSIS AND TREATMENT, ALTHOUGH THE PRIME RESPONSIBILITY FOR RECOVERY REMAINS WITH THE AFFECTED PERSON.

BALANCING ENERGY FLOW

Shamans often use a feather fan to clean the subtle energy field of the patient. They smudge the patient, and then use the fan, or sometimes an entire dried bird wing, to cleanse the energy of the person, freeing areas of blocked or sluggish energy, and removing excess energy from places that need draining. The feathers become the tools of the intent of the shamans, who feel deep into the patient with their awareness.

A rattle can be used in much the same way as a feather. Hold it above the patient, and shake the rattle over them, feeling the way the rattle moves, and sensing the energy of the patient through it. Rattles are especially good at this, which is why some shamans favor them as diagnostic tools.

HERBAL TREATMENT

Herbal remedies are sometimes part of shamanic treatment, but proper training is essential, because some herbs can be dangerous if given incorrectly.

CLEARING ENERGY FIELDS

1 Use a large single feather or a group of large feathers. Bind their quills in red to protect yourself.

2 Smudge yourself, the patient, and the feathers.

3 Move the feathers over the patient's body, sensing the sick person's energy as you do so.

4 Some areas may suggest to you that they need special attention, such as flicking or hitting with the feather, to free up the energy. Follow your intuition rather than your head.

5 Work systematically over the entire body until you feel that you have smoothed out any disruptions to the patient's energy flow.

6 Let the patient rest.

A shaman from Zambia treating his patient.

DEVELOPING
SHAMANIC AWARENESS

YOUR SHAMANIC AWARENESS IS LIKE AN INNER EYE THROUGH WHICH YOU SEE THE WORLD DIFFERENTLY. IT MAY RESEMBLE A DEEP SENSE OF KNOWING, OR A PROFOUND AWARENESS OF THE BALANCE OR IMBALANCE OF A SITUATION.

PATHS TO PERCEPTION

You will find your own shamanic awareness through practice and experience. The best method is to put yourself into sacred situations, such as ceremonies and sacred spaces, to perform shamanic rituals, and to reflect upon your own medicine.

Another good practice is to go into the wild places of our earth with the intent that you are there for a sacred purpose. These places give you a chance to be quietly by yourself, and to interact with the world in an unhurried and uncluttered way. Remember to approach wild places with a physical as well as a sacred respect, and do not put yourself into situations that are beyond your ability. The land can be a great teacher, but it may not be gentle if you take foolish risks.

EVERYDAY AWARENESS

Everything in this world is alive and related to you, so every place you go to gives you the opportunity to perceive the world from a sacred viewpoint. Develop your awareness in your everyday life. As you walk down a street, try to sense the flow of energy along it. Do the same when you walk in the park; the land is alive even when it is filled with other people. Do not be too serious about it. Just tread lightly and explore the energy perceptions that you normally ignore.

HOW TO PROMOTE AWARENESS

- Create, tend, and work with shrines or altars.
- Practice rituals for the psychic protection of your space.
- Perform smudging.
- Take part in ceremonies.
- Make sacred craftwork from an intuitive perspective.
- Reflect on your own medicine and nature.
- Go into wild natural places with a sacred intent.
- Open your senses to the energy that flows through everything around you.

You can follow a sacred path in an urban environment as well as in the countryside.

WORKING WITH
ANIMAL SPIRITS

A RELATIONSHIP WITH ANIMAL SPIRITS IS ONE OF THE OLDEST ELEMENTS OF SHAMANISM. MANY SHAMANS HAVE ANIMAL SPIRIT HELPERS THAT TEACH, PROTECT, AND GUIDE THEM. THE RELATIONSHIP THAT A SHAMAN DEVELOPS WITH AN ANIMAL SPIRIT HELPER CAN BE A MAJOR INFLUENCE IN THE PERFORMANCE OF SACRED TASKS.

YOUR ANIMAL HELPER

According to some shamanic traditions, everyone has animal helpers, without which they cannot live. If you are unaware of them, you are simply not in touch with them in a conscious way. Some people's spirit animals are foxes, wolves, or bears. Others have less predatory animals, such as rabbits, deer, or elk. You cannot easily predict which animal will work with you, and you cannot order an animal to do so; remember that an animal spirit is a separate entity, and the right one will come to you at the right time.

BLOWING IN

Perhaps the best way to meet your spirit animal is to find someone who can drum you along a shamanic journey to the lower world. There you can call to an animal, and if it comes to you, you can bring it back to this world, where the shaman will blow it into you. This "blowing in" of power—generally to the head and the heart—is one of the ways shamans put power or spiritual knowledge into people.

Even without the benefit of a drum journey, however, you may have a deep sense of an animal always being around you. You may know what this animal spirit is, or you may need to reflect upon it. An animal may keep appearing unexpectedly in this physical life; crows may always come and perch near you, for example, or foxes may cross your path in unexpected places. That could be your animal spirit helper.

Our relatives in the animal world are all around us and always ready to teach us.

Take care when choosing your animal helper. Creatures like the badger will bring both their positive and negative attributes to you.

GETTING ACQUAINTED

When you have a good idea what your spirit animal helper is, you can begin to work with it in your life. You can ask it to be with you in situations that are difficult for you. But one word of caution—the animal will bring its characteristics to the situation. If you work with a badger, for example, and you call the badger to you, be careful not to badger people aggressively and override their points of view. It is essential to examine the background of your animal, from both a zoological and a folklore perspective. This will give you greater knowledge about the animal—and probably also about yourself.

DEVELOPING A RELATIONSHIP

You may be able to obtain the animal's bones, teeth, claws, or fur to make a bundle (see page 81) to keep near you. Or you could place photos or representations of the animal on your altar. Try making a fetish statue of the animal; however crude the art, it is your intent that matters. A horse fetish can be a simple wooden stick with horsehair tied to it; if it says horse to you, then it is a horse—you are the sole judge.

Keep fetishes of your animal near you to develop a relationship with it. A fetish can be a figurative sculpture, such as this bear and snake, or simply a piece of fur or skin wrapped around a wooden stick.

Talk to your animal, call to it, and have it around you. Be aware of it with your inner vision, and sense when it is there and when it is not. In this way you will develop a close working relationship with the animal spirit that will benefit your shamanic practice.

BEING WITH THE LAND

THE LAND THAT YOU WALK UPON IS A SACRED PLACE. WHEREVER YOU LIVE, THE LAND WAS HELD SACRED BY PEOPLE WHO PASSED BEFORE YOU AND WHO MADE IT HOME TO THEIR SACRED SITES. BE RESPECTFUL WHERE YOU WALK, AND LEAVE OFFERINGS TO THE ANCESTORS; ONE DAY IN THE NOT TOO DISTANT FUTURE, YOU TOO WILL BE AN ANCESTOR.

Some sacred sites are imposing; they are ancient standing stones, mounds, and painted rocks. Others are less apparent, but no less sacred. These are caves, hills, valleys, waterfalls, or woods. Wherever you go, tread with respect for the beauty of the world. Do no damage, and take only what you need, leaving a gift as you do.

Standing stones, such as the pillars of limestone in the Pinnacles Desert in Australia, are imposing sacred sites.

VISITING A SACRED PLACE

If you come to an extraordinary sacred place, ask the spirit's permission to be there; do not rush in blindly. Take a moment to touch the earth, and say, "Thank you for this beautiful place," and leave an offering as an entrance gift. This can be a tiny thing, such as a hair from your head.

Use such places to pray in. Respect others who do not share your ways. You do not need to arrive in a place and perform a showy ceremony to proclaim what a powerful shaman you are. Just do what you do quietly, so that others do not notice. If you have the chance to be alone with a sacred place, you can be more elaborate—you could sing to the spirits of the place, or make offering and prayers to each of the four directions.

Whatever you do and wherever you go, walk with your awareness ready to perceive the subtle energy of the place you are in. Be quiet and respectful. These sites have been there for eons, and will no doubt remain longer than you can imagine. You are just a small visitor in a living landscape.

The beauty of the world shows its spirit to us, often in dramatic ways.

FINDING VISION

NATURE IS THE GREATEST TEACHER. MANY CULTURES HAVE A "VISION QUEST":
A TIME SPENT ALONE IN NATURE PRAYING AND SEEKING INSTRUCTION FROM THE
SPIRITS THAT ARE ALL AROUND US.

THE VISION QUEST

The term "vision quest" derives from
the Native American Lakota *Hanblecheya*
(He cried for a vision). The Native American
vision quest is a ceremony that normally
lasts for three to four days but can
continue for up to nine. During this time,
the seeker goes without food and water
while praying on a hill. While the seeker is
on the hill, he or she receives the teachings
of the land and the spirits.

THE MEDICINE WALK

A less extreme way of entering into
dialogue with the land is to take a
medicine walk. This means going out
ceremonially on a walk, in the country or
the town, to experience all that you can
and to learn from it. Try to find time to
sit for an hour or so in a quiet, secluded
place—to enter, in a very small way, the
empty dreamlike place of the full vision
quest. Let the world of the spirits give you
all you need to learn at this time.

TAKING A MEDICINE WALK

1 Set out with a sacred intent.

2 Abstain from food and drink
throughout the walk.

3 Start and end the walk with
a specific ritual, such as passing
through a gate or stepping over
a wooden bar. Once you cross the
threshold, you are in sacred time,
and the world will teach you.

4 Avoid contact with people,
and any talk.

5 Gently dispel busy distractions.

6 During the walk, sit silently for
about an hour in a secluded place.

7 Be aware of your footsteps, and
of everything that you experience,
and let the world of the spirits lighten
and enlighten you.

Take a medicine walk to explore
and learn from the land.

DREAMING

HAVE YOU EVER DREAMED A DREAM SO REAL THAT YOU KNOW IT IS SPECIAL? PERHAPS AN ANIMAL, OR A PERSON YOU KNEW TO BE DEAD, CAME AND SPOKE TO YOU. PERHAPS YOU WERE SHOWN SOMETHING THAT WAS GOING TO HAPPEN. THIS KIND OF DREAM IS A "MEDICINE DREAM."

THE IMPORTANCE OF DREAMS

Shamans of many cultures actively encourage dreams to occur by means of dreaming bundles and ceremonies. Dreams are also considered potentially dangerous by some cultures. They believe it is important to act out the dreams in this world in a controlled way to prevent them from taking control of the dreamer. Other cultures regard the dream as the real world, and this world as the dream world, so for them, dreams are crucial.

USING YOUR DREAMS

We all dream, although we do not always remember our dreams. Try putting a notebook or tape recorder by your bed, so that you can record your dreams the moment you wake up. Dreaming is a way to knowledge that works better for some people than for others. If it is your way, explore it and learn all it has to show you, but if it does not appeal to you, find other ways to seek wisdom.

A DREAMING BUNDLE

Help to summon dreams with a dreaming bundle, which acts as a container for your dreaming intent. Make the bundle from a red cloth bag, and place it on your personal altar, or hang it by your bed when you wish to dream. The bag should contain the following items:

- An object, such as a feather, that represents an owl, a bird of the night, associated with dreaming.
- An object that represents a bear, whose hibernating habit helped to earn it the title of keeper of the dream.
- A turquoise gemstone, associated with the sky and dreaming.
- Some sage for protection.
- A small quartz crystal to focus intent and to amplify it.

The dreamscapes of our sleep are a rich place to receive teachings and knowledge to aid our shamanic practice.

FOLLOWING A SHAMANIC PATH

IF YOU ARE INTRIGUED BY WHAT YOU READ HERE AND WISH TO DEVELOP YOUR SHAMANIC SKILLS, THERE ARE TEACHERS WHO CAN SHOW YOU WAYS TO CONNECT WITH THE SPIRITS. ALWAYS BE OPEN TO LEARNING FROM DIFFERENT TEACHERS; NO ONE SHAMAN HAS ALL OF THE ANSWERS.

ONE TRADITION, MANY TEACHERS

You may find a teacher who has a good knowledge of ceremony, or another with special healing skills. It is not advisable to pick and mix different paths, however. A good grounding in one tradition will give you a secure platform from which to develop your shamanic understandings.

There are many shamanic paths open to you, with workshops and books about Native American, Celtic, and Mongolian shamanism, and a host of others. Explore your chosen path as you wish—each has much to teach—but keep your own shamanic practice simple. You do not need to attend one powerful ceremony after another, trying to experience "the real thing." Many shamans are quiet people, who just do what they do without any commotion.

You could keep a medicine bundle in your car to develop your shamanic awareness.

PRAYER AND GRATITUDE

Learn about ceremony, and if it appeals to you, you can gain the knowledge to hold ceremonies yourself. You may find yourself drawn to a specific ceremonial path, such as working with the Native American sacred pipe. Bear in mind at all times that this is not a gimmick—it is a sacred path that was traveled by many people before you—and give it the honor it deserves.

The best teachings will come if you are humble and ask the spirits to help you learn. Develop your awareness, but be wary of launching into flights of fantasy. Shamanism is a grounded spirituality that is, in essence, about prayer and gratitude for the gift of life.

The shaman's path is the path of humanity—we are all related.

BECOMING A **REAL HUMAN BEING**

Maybe you have been collecting feathers and pinecones for years, your house is filled with stones and bits of driftwood from past vacations, and you love to be in wild places—now maybe you are wondering what to do next.

A Path with a Heart

The many teachers offering courses will teach you about animism, and all will be Natives, because we are all natives of this beautiful earth. Some will have much to impart, and some will say that they are just two-legged creatures who do not know much, and that maybe you know things that they do not.

Being a human being, however, is not about the next course you are taking; it is about following a path with a heart. There are lifetimes of learning for you out in the world with all of your relations, learning to be a human being by being with the wind, the water, the owl, and the squirrel.

All Your Relations

As you go on your path, you will make mistakes; we all do. There will be times when you think you know so much, and discover that you know so very little. The spirits will go with you as you learn, and if you respect them and are open to the simple things they teach you, you will gain knowledge from them.

You will learn to walk gratefully on the earth, respecting yourself as a sacred being, and all

others as sacred beings on the same sacred hoop. You will know when you are right without having the need to prove it, and step lightly on the knowledge of others, so as not to hurt it. You will know how to prepare and conduct a ceremony, to help a sick friend, or to give direction to those who are lost. And when you are doing these things, your face will be turned toward being a human being—and the spirits will be with you.

The beauty of the natural world can give us great power.

When we become aware of the wonder of the world, we can truly live in a spiritual way.

FURTHER READING
AND RESOURCES

SHAMANISM IN GENERAL

The Shaman
Piers Vitebsky
Macmillan Books
ISBN 0-333-63847-6

Shamanism
Nevill Drury
Element Books
ISBN 1-85230-794-3

Shamanism—Archaic Techniques of Ecstasy
Mircea Eliade
Penguin Books
ISBN 0-14-019155-0

Shamans
Tampere Museums
ISBN 951-609-070-2

Voices From the Earth
Nicholas Wood
Sterling Books/Godsfield Press
ISBN 0-8069-6609-2

The Way of the Animal Powers
Joseph Campbell
Times Books
ISBN 0-7230-0256-8

NATIVE AMERICAN TRADITIONS

Fools Crow Wisdom and Power
Thomas E. Mails
Council Oak Books
ISBN 0-933031-35-1

Mother Earth Spirituality
Ed McGaa Eagle Man
HarperSanFrancisco
ISBN 0-06-250596-3

Secrets of the Talking Jaguar
Martin Prechtel
Element Books
ISBN 1-86204-501-1

Soul Retrieval
Sandra Ingerman
HarperSanFrancisco
ISBN 0-06-250406-1

Yuwipi
William K. Powers
University of Nebraska Press
ISBN 0-8032-8710-0

US RESOURCES

Dance of the Deer
  Foundation
PO Box 699
Soquel, CA 95073
www.shamanism.com
Tel: (831) 475 9560

The Foundation for
  Shamanic Studies
PO Box 1939
Mill Valley, CA 94942
www.shamanism.org
Tel: (415) 380 8282

Jaya Bear
PO Box 1950
El Prado, NM 87529
www.spiritjourneys.net
Tel: (505) 758 1491

Johnny Moses
PO Box 1210
LaConner, WA 98257
www.johnnymoses.com
Tel: (206) 860 7885

Ojai Foundation
9739 Ojai-Santa
   Paula Road
Ojai, CA 93023
Tel: (805) 646 8343
Email: Ojaifdn@
   jetlink.net

Sacred Circles Institute
PO Box 733
Mukilteo, WA 98275
Tel: (425) 353 8815
Email: mattie@seanet.com

UK RESOURCES

Centre for Shamanic
   Studies
29 Chambers Lane
London NW10 2JR
Tel: (020) 8459 3028

Eagles Wing Centre
58 Westbere Road
London NW2 3RU
www.shamanism.co.uk
Tel: (020) 7435 8174
Email: eagleswing@
   shamanism.co.uk

Sacred Hoop Magazine
PO Box 16
Narberth
West Wales SA67 8YG
www.sacredhoop.
   demon.co.uk
Tel: (01834) 860320
Email: Mail@sacredhoop.
   demon.co.uk
The Pathways Centre, which
provides shamanic training and
ceremonial objects, also operates
from the above address

The Sacred Trust
PO Box 603
Bath BA1 2ZU
Tel: (01225) 852615
Email: SacredTrust@
   compuserve.com

Spirit Talk—A Core
   Shamanic Newsletter
120 Argyle Street
Cambridge CB1 3LQ
www.users.dircon.
   co.uk/~snail
Tel: (01223) 562838
Email: kkelly@caci.co.uk

Wilderness Quest
1 Green Court
Middle Yard
Kings Stanley
Stone House
Glos GL10 3QH
Tel: (01453) 828645

INDEX

CREDITS

Quarto would like to thank and acknowledge the following
for supplying pictures reproduced in this book:

p7 Peter Waldal/The Image Bank; p9 Jan Peder Flood; p10 (person) Pictor International, London; p12 A. Kuznetsov/Trip; p13 (above) J-L Charmet; p13 (below) Pictures Colour Library; p14 Pictures Colour Library; p16 (left) David W. Hamilton/The Image Bank; p16 (right) R. Belbin/Trip; p17 (above left) Pictures Colour Library; p17 (above right) J-L Charmet; p17 (below) B. Vikander/Trip; p20 J-L Charmet; p21 (main image) Pictor International, London; p23 Pictor International, London; p25 (above left & below) Avner Ofer; p25 (above right) Jan Peder Flood; pp26-27 (main image) Pictures Colour Library; p27 (inset left) Michael Melford/The Image Bank; p28 American Heritage Center, University of Wyoming; p29 Pictor International, London; p31 (below) Pictor International, London; p32 Steve Murez/The Image Bank; p33 Pictor International, London; p41 (tree) Pictor International, London; p43 Heather Angel; p44 Jan Peder Flood; p45 (below) the art archive; p46 Heather Angel; p55 Jan Peder Flood; p56 (main image) Heather Angel; p56 (inset right) Michael Melford/The Image Bank; p58 J-L Charmet; p59 C. Gray/Trip; p60 Jan Peder Flood; p66 the art archive; p71 (above) the art archive; p75 Heather Angel; p77 Grant V. Faint/The Image Bank; p85 Heather Angel; p89 Pictures Colour Library; p91 A. Kuznetsov/Trip; p93 J-L Charmet; p106 C. Treppe/Trip; p109 (group of people) Andrew Yates/ The Image Bank; p111 Jason Venus/Natural Visions; p112 Pictor International, London; p119 (central image of feathers) Pictor International, London; p121 A. Kuznetsov/Trip

All other photographs and illustrations are the copyright of Quarto.

While every effort has been made to credit contributors, Quarto would like
to apologize should there have been any omissions or errors.